Writers Uncovered

C.S. LEWIS

Vic Parker

Heinemann
LIBRARY

www.heinemann.co.uk/library
Visit our website to find out more information about Heinemann Library books.

To order:
☎ Phone 44 (0) 1865 888066
📄 Send a fax to 44 (0) 1865 314091
🖥 Visit the Heinemann bookshop at www.heinemann.co.uk/library to browse
our catalogue and order online.

First published in Great Britain by
Heinemann Library, Halley Court, Jordan Hill,
Oxford OX2 8EJ, part of Harcourt Education.

Heinemann is a registered trademark of
Harcourt Education Ltd.

Editorial: Charlotte Guillain and Dave Harris
Design: Richard Parker and Q2A Solutions
Picture research: Hannah Taylor and
    Andrea Sadler
Production: Duncan Gilbert

Originated by Chroma Graphics (O) Pte Ltd.
Printed and bound in China by
    South China Printing Company

10 digit ISBN: 0 431 90627 0
13 digit ISBN: 978 0 431 90627 0

10 09 08 07 06
10 9 8 7 6 5 4 3 2 1

British Library Cataloguing in Publication Data
Parker, Vic
   C.S. Lewis. – (Writers uncovered)
   823.9'12
A full catalogue record for this book is
available from the British Library.

Acknowledgements
The publishers would like to thank the
following for permission to reproduce
photographs:
CILIP p. **36**; Getty Images pp. **13**, **20** (Time
Life Pictures), **39**; Harcourt Brace Jovanovich
p. **7**; Harcourt Education Ltd p. **42** (Tudor
Photography); HarperCollins p. **19**; Kobal
Collection p. **23** (Shadowlands/Spelling/
Price/Savoy); Mary Evans Picture Library
pp. **8**, **15**, **24**; National Portrait Gallery p. **27**
(Arthur Strong); Photodisc p. **26**; Robbie Jack
p. **37**; The Art Archive p. **9** (The Bodleian
Library); Topham Picturepoint p. **17**; Used
by permission of The Marion E. Wade Center,
Wheaton College, Wheaton, IL. pp. **4**, **6**, **10**,
11, **12**, **14**, **16**, **22**, **25**, **29**, **30**, **31**, **32**, **33**,
35, **34**, **21**.

Every effort has been made to contact
copyright holders of any material reproduced
in this book. Any omissions will be rectified
in subsequent printings if notice is given to
the publishers.

The paper used to print this book comes
from sustainable resources.

CONTENTS

Words appearing in the text in bold, **like this**, are explained in the glossary.

THE GENIUS BEHIND NARNIA

Have you ever looked inside a wardrobe to check if there is a way into another world? This is the mark of a true fan of *The Chronicles of Narnia* – the classic children's **fantasy** series by C.S. Lewis. Lewis was a university professor at Oxford and Cambridge. He wrote his famous series of seven tales in the early 1950s: *The Magician's Nephew*; *The Lion, the Witch and the Wardrobe*; *The Horse and his Boy*; *Prince Caspian*; *The Voyage of the Dawn Treader*; *The Silver Chair*; and *The Last Battle*. Millions of young readers have since been captivated by the magical world of Narnia that he created. It is a world where you can talk to lions, beavers, and witches, and where years pass by in the blink of an eye.

This is the face behind the stories.

What was C.S. Lewis like?

Lewis was a big man with a large red face and a booming voice. He once wrote: "My happiest hours are spent with three or four old friends in old clothes tramping together … or else sitting up till the small hours in someone's college rooms talking".

As a teenager, Lewis loved collecting copies of his favourite stories and poetry. However, when he was a young man, money was often tight, so he rarely spent any on books. Instead, he memorized long passages off by heart. He also had a huge knowledge of ancient languages, including old Icelandic, Welsh, French, German, and Italian, as well as Greek, Latin, and both Old and **Medieval** English. Besides writing *The Chronicles of Narnia*, Lewis wrote many thought-provoking books for adults.

FIND OUT MORE...

Here are some of C.S. Lewis's favourites:

Favourite animal...	Lewis loved animals, in particular a pet terrier called Mr Papworth.
Favourite hobbies...	Chatting about literature, playing with words and language.
Favourite music...	Wagner's *The Ring*.
Favourite novel...	Lewis thought that Leo Tolstoy's *War and Peace* was the greatest novel ever written.
Favourite holiday...	Walking tours in Britain and Ireland, often with his brother.
Favourite friends...	J.R.R. Tolkien, author of *The Hobbit* and *The Lord of the Rings*, and Roger Lancelyn Green, author of fantasy and **myths** for young people.

LEWIS GROWS UP

Clive Staples Lewis was born on 29 November 1898, in Belfast, Northern Ireland. His mother, Flora, was a very intelligent woman who had obtained two mathematics **degrees** at Queen's University in Belfast. His father, Albert, was a **lawyer** with his own firm. Clive had an elder brother, Warren Hamilton, who had been born almost three-and-a-half years earlier. The two boys became devoted friends as they grew up together.

Choosing his own name

One day when Clive was four, he announced out of the blue that he wanted to be known as Jacksie. He told everyone firmly that he would no longer answer to Clive. Jacksie gradually became shortened to Jack, which is what family and friends called him for the rest of his life. Similarly, Warren decided that he wanted to be called Warnie.

The young "Jacksie" wearing a sailor suit, which was fashionable for boys at the time.

An inspiring house

When Lewis was six, the family moved to a house on the edge of the city, surrounded by countryside. Lewis and his brother often enjoyed days out exploring on their bicycles. Lewis also loved the house itself, which was called Little Lea. It was huge and rambling with unexpected corridors, rooms and spaces to explore, such as passages to scramble through in the roof.

HAVE A GO

Lewis used one of Little Lea's attics as a study for writing stories about animals who had adventures in a land called Boxen. He drew his characters wearing clothes, rather like the animals in Beatrix Potter tales, which he loved.

Think about your own story involving animals. Would your characters wear clothes? Would they talk? What kind of world would they live in, and what adventures would they have?

Lewis's childhood stories were published in this book in 1985.

BOXEN

THE IMAGINARY WORLD OF ·THE YOUNG· **C.S.LEWIS**

EDITED BY WALTER HOOPER

Books, books, and more books

Lewis's parents filled Little Lea with books. Lewis adored stories. As a very young child, his Irish nanny told him ancient **Celtic** fairytales. As he grew up, Lewis was enchanted by magical tales from E. Nesbit, such as *The Amulet*. He was also fascinated by tales of heroes, such as medieval knights and a Roman slave called Ben Hur. He became interested in Viking legends and other myths after reading *Siegfried and the Twilight of the Gods*, illustrated by Arthur Rackham.

Lewis was inspired by dramatic illustrations like this one from *Siegfried and the Twilight of the Gods* by Margaret Armour.

This is a page of a Medieval English book by Geoffrey Chaucer, who was one of the writers Lewis studied.

School life

Lewis was first taught at home by a **governess**. When he was nearly ten, his mother became ill and died. Lewis was then sent to boarding school in England with his brother. Wynyard School, Hertfordshire, was a brutal place with a cruel headmaster. Lewis hated it. His father soon transferred the boys to Cherbourg school in Malvern. Lewis became very good at English and Latin, and won an entrance prize called a **scholarship** to Malvern College. He then went to a private tutor in Surrey, Mr Kirkpatrick, to specialize in all sorts of literature including Ancient Greek, Medieval English, and Shakespeare. This inspired Lewis to start writing poetry. At the age of eighteen, he won a scholarship to Oxford University.

FIND OUT MORE...

No one guided Lewis's reading. When he was eighteen he stumbled upon a story called *Phantastes*. Lewis had discovered a leading children's fantasy writer, George Macdonald, who became one of his all-time favourite authors. He did not discover Kenneth Grahame's *The Wind in the Willows* until he was in his twenties.

SOLDIER, STUDENT, SCHOLAR

Lewis went to University College, part of Oxford University, in April 1917. As he started his studies he also trained as an army officer. All young men in Britain were needed to fight overseas in World War I. Lewis became firm friends with his roommate, Paddy Moore. Moore was also from Northern Ireland, and his mother and sister had come to live near him in Oxford. Lewis and Moore made a solemn promise that if one of them died in the war, the other would look after their family.

FIND OUT MORE...

World War I lasted from 1914 to 1918. It came about because of tensions that had been growing for many years between two sets of European **allies**: Germany, Austria, and Hungary on one side, and Britain, France, and Russia on the other. It is sometimes called "the Great War" because around 15 million people died, and it involved more countries at a larger scale than any other war before.

This picture shows Lewis (on the left) and Moore (on the right) before they went to war.

Living dangerously

On 17 November 1917, Lewis was sent to fight in mud-filled **trenches** in France. The soldiers were bombarded continually by bombs and machine-gun fire, and many of them were injured or killed. In March 1918, Lewis himself was wounded in the arm, chest, and leg, and he was sent back to hospital in England. Lewis knew he was very lucky to be alive. While he slowly recovered, he put together a collection of his poems and sent them to a publishing company.

The legacy of war

The war ended in November 1918, and in January the next year Lewis returned to university to study **Classics**. He was thrilled when just two months later, his poems were published as a book called *Spirits in Bondage*. However, times were also sad. Paddy Moore never came home from the war because he had been killed.

C.S. Lewis the university student, photographed in 1919 at age 20.

Student life

Lewis kept his vow and began giving money to Mrs Moore, who was still in lodgings in Oxford with her daughter. This caused a row with Lewis's father, who was supporting him financially. However, Lewis's father continued his allowance, and in June 1921 Lewis rented a house for himself and the Moores to share. Meanwhile, Lewis did well with his studies, and also won an English essay prize. He decided he wanted to be a university teacher, writing poetry in his spare time.

Top results

In August 1922, Lewis finished his Classics degree with the top grade that was rarely awarded, called a Double First. The following year he crammed in an English degree that would usually take three years, and also gained a First in that! Lewis began work as a temporary tutor at University College in Oxford. In 1925, another part of Oxford University, called Magdalen College, offered him a permanent English teaching position called a Fellowship.

C.S. Lewis with his colleagues at Magdalen College in Oxford. Lewis is on the back row, sixth from the left.

Lewis the lecturer

Lewis continued to keep a home with the Moores but was also given rooms in Magdalen College in which to teach, study, and write. University teaching was hard work and, together with his family responsibilities, Lewis at first found it difficult to fit in much writing. However, he did have a long poem called *Dymer* published in September 1926, and over the next couple of years he began other projects, such as a poem called *The King of Drum*, a novel, and an **academic** book on medieval literature and life.

FIND OUT MORE...

From 1926, Lewis went to meetings of "the Coalbiters' Club", a group which read Old Icelandic literature. He became great friends with the club's founder, J.R.R. Tolkien. Tolkien was also a university teacher, who later became world-famous as author of *The Hobbit*, *The Lord of the Rings*, and *The Silmarillion*.

J.R.R. Tolkien was an extremely talented teacher and writer, just like his friend Lewis.

The end of an era

On 25 September 1929, Lewis's elderly father died. Lewis and his brother, Warnie, undertook the sad task of clearing out Little Lea so it could be sold. When the brothers came across their old toy trunk, they could not bring themselves to look inside. They buried it, unopened, in the vegetable patch.

A new start

Warnie was an officer in the army. After many years overseas, he was now returning to Britain. With money from the sale of Little Lea, Lewis and Warnie bought a big, beautiful house for themselves and the Moores to live in: The Kilns, on the outskirts of Oxford. It was tucked away at the end of a lane and had a meadow, wood, lake, and tennis court. They all moved in on 11 October 1930. Two years later, Warnie retired from the army altogether.

The Kilns was Lewis's home for the rest of his life.

An important turning point

After Lewis lost his father, he thought deeply about life and death. He had close friends who were Christians, such as J.R.R. Tolkien, and Lewis also developed a strong faith. In August 1932, he wrote a book about finding Christianity: *The Pilgrim's Regress*. Then Lewis embarked on a massive project which would take him years to complete, a book on 16th-century writing for the Oxford History of English Literature. Meanwhile, Lewis finished his book on medieval life and literature. Published in 1936, *The **Allegory** of Love* was a huge success in the academic world and made his name as a writer.

INSIDE INFORMATION

An allegory is a piece of writing that has a hidden layer of meaning as well as a more obvious meaning. Lewis's book *The Pilgrim's Regress* was an allegory based on his religious beliefs. He named it after another famous allegory: *The Pilgrim's Progress*, written by John Bunyan in the 17th century.

This map shows the main character's journey in John Bunyan's book *The Pilgrim's Progress*.

A LIFE OF WRITING AND TEACHING

Lewis often met up with his friend, J.R.R. Tolkien, to show each other their writing and discuss their thoughts. Lewis greatly admired the children's book Tolkien started writing, *The Hobbit*. Other writer friends sometimes joined them, and by the mid 1930s, a small group was meeting regularly at the Eagle and Child pub on Tuesday mornings and in Lewis's college rooms on Thursday evenings.

The friends called themselves "the Inklings". Lewis and Tolkien shared strong feelings about literature. They thought that many contemporary stories were not as good as ancient myths. They set themselves a challenge: to write modern myths, disguised as thrillers. Tolkien wrote a time-travel story called *The Lost Road*, while Lewis wrote a **science-fiction** story with a Christian background, called *Out of the Silent Planet*. It was published in 1938 and was well received.

Lewis continued to meet with members of the Inklings later in life.

War time

In 1939, World War II broke out. Britain and other nations sent their armed forces to fight in Europe, to stop Germany invading other countries. Lewis was 40, but as he had been injured in World War I he did not go to fight this time. Instead, he joined a part-time organization known as the Home Guard, who were preparing in case the Germans invaded Britain. Meanwhile, Lewis continued teaching at the university, although few students were left. He also took in three schoolgirl **evacuees** at The Kilns. He tried writing stories to entertain them, but he did not get very far with his ideas.

FIND OUT MORE...

The Home Guard was made up of many men in the UK during World War II who were not in the army, but volunteered to help protect the country. Some of them had fought in World War I. They did not have many weapons or supplies, but they still prepared to fight if the country was invaded.

These Home Guard volunteer soldiers are training with pieces of wood instead of weapons.

Inspiring others

During the long, terrible years of the war, which lasted until 1945, Lewis did a lot of thinking on what life is all about. He wrote a book about human suffering called *The Problem of Pain*, which was published in October 1940. Producers at the BBC were impressed with the book, and asked Lewis to do a series of radio broadcasts speaking about life, death, and God. These were later published as a book called *Mere Christianity*.

Giving advice

Lewis was asked by the Royal Air Force to give talks at their bases, and was also sometimes asked to give speeches in churches. He became very well known, and people began writing to him to ask advice on all sorts of emotional problems. This continued for the rest of his life, and Lewis spent hours writing very careful, caring replies.

Different types of writing

Even before *The Problem of Pain* appeared in print, Lewis was hard at work on other projects. An idea for a work of **fiction** came to him in church one Sunday in July 1940: a collection of letters written from an elderly, retired devil, Screwtape, to his young, inexperienced nephew, a junior devil called Wormwood. These letters were hugely entertaining, as well as thought-provoking.

At the same time, Lewis wrote an academic preface to the great poem *Paradise Lost* by John Milton. Lewis also wrote a sequel to his science-fiction novel *Out of the Silent Planet*, called *Perelandra*.

INSIDE INFORMATION

When *The Screwtape Letters* appeared in *The Guardian* newspaper, Lewis was paid £2 per letter and gave all the money to charity. When the letters were published as a book, Lewis made a lot of money. He decided to give away two-thirds of all his profits, putting the money into a special charity trust fund.

A breakthrough book

Lewis's Screwtape and Wormwood correspondence was published in serial form in *The Guardian* newspaper from May to November 1941, then as a book in the UK in February 1942, and in the USA in 1943.

The Screwtape Letters flew off the bookshop shelves and it was reprinted time after time. It immediately became a best-seller and Lewis found himself suddenly famous internationally. People who had never heard of his previous books now started devouring those too. Lewis received so many letters that Warnie started working as his secretary, handling the business side of Lewis's writing.

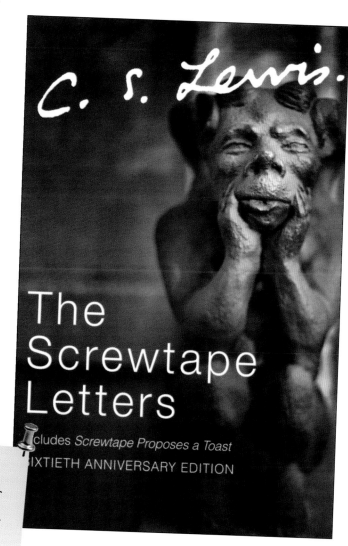

C. S. Lewis.

The Screwtape Letters

Includes *Screwtape Proposes a Toast*

SIXTIETH ANNIVERSARY EDITION

The Screwtape Letters have never stopped selling well. This is a 60th anniversary edition.

A busy life

Lewis's home life was difficult. Mrs Moore's daughter, Maureen, got married and left The Kilns, but Mrs Moore herself became elderly and ill. She needed a lot of help and support. Warnie also began to sink into depression and alcoholism. However, all sorts of writing flooded from Lewis's pen: a third and final science-fiction novel, *That Hideous Strength* (1945); a book called *The Great Divorce* (1946) which was inspired by the Italian writer Dante's *The Divine Comedy*; and a book exploring miracles (1947). By the autumn of 1947, Lewis was such a famous writer that he appeared on the front cover of a leading American magazine, *Time*. The following year, at the age of 49, he began writing his life story, which was later published as a book called *Surprised by Joy*.

It was a great honour for Lewis to be pictured on the front cover of *Time* magazine.

A brand new direction

Meanwhile, Lewis's old friend J.R.R. Tolkien was working on an **epic** creation, called *The Lord of the Rings*. A student friend, Roger Lancelyn Green, was also creating a children's fantasy story, where four main characters stray into a strange wood, cut off from time. Lewis himself tried once more to write children's stories.

By March 1949 he had finished a tale called *The Lion, the Witch and the Wardrobe*, set in the magical world of Narnia. It took him just five years to write a series of seven stories, *The Chronicles of Narnia*. Sales grew steadily all over the world, until the books became children's classics.

INSIDE INFORMATION

Tolkien really disliked Lewis's Narnia tales, but Roger Lancelyn Green greatly admired them. He made comments on each one which Lewis found very helpful. Green later became a successful, highly-respected children's author himself. He also wrote a biography about Lewis.

Lewis was at his happiest when he was writing.

On the move

In 1951, Mrs Moore died. The following year, Lewis finally finished the book he had undertaken nine years earlier on 16th-century writing. When in 1954 a vacancy arose at Cambridge University for a Professor of Medieval and **Renaissance** English, Lewis was free to accept the new challenge. From January 1955, Lewis lived at Magdalene College, Cambridge, during the week and returned to The Kilns for weekends and vacations.

Lewis gets married

One of the many fans who regularly wrote to Lewis was an American poet called Joy Davidman. She came to England with her two sons in Autumn 1952, and she and Lewis struck up a close friendship. After three years, Lewis offered to help Joy by marrying her so she could stay in England permanently. They had a legal ceremony in April 1956 and continued to live separately, as friends.

Joy Davidman was 37 when she met Lewis, after her first marriage had broken down.

The story of Lewis and Joy's relationship was later turned into a stage play, a television drama, and a 1994 film, *Shadowlands*.

The movie *Shadowlands* starred Anthony Hopkins as Lewis and Debra Winger as Joy.

Tragic times

As usual, Lewis was busy working on several projects, including a novel set in Ancient Greece called *Till We Have Faces*. However, in October, disaster struck. Joy was discovered to have **cancer** and given only a few months to live.

By April 1957, she was gravely ill, but she stunned everyone by slowly recovering. As she did so, Lewis found himself at last falling in love with her. The couple went on holiday to Ireland in July, and shared over a year of happiness together at The Kilns before Joy fell ill again in October 1959. In spite of this, Joy and Lewis went on a wonderful holiday to Greece in April 1960. In July, Joy died.

Final writings

To get through his bereavement, 61-year-old Lewis threw himself into writing. The result was a book called *A Grief Observed*. *The Saturday Evening Post* newspaper asked if he would write more Screwtape letters, and Lewis created a new instalment called *Screwtape Proposes a Toast*. He then wrote a new introduction so that the original letters and *Screwtape Proposes a Toast* could be published in one book.

Lewis also wrote an academic book, called *An Experiment in Criticism*. However, in the summer of 1961, Lewis was forced to slow down. He became ill with a series of problems, which affected his kidneys and his heart. He had to take time off from university teaching and relax at The Kilns. He had Joy's two sons and Warnie for company, and he read endlessly.

INSIDE INFORMATION

All sorts of personal passions influenced Lewis during his long writing career. The Narnia stories contain elements of his Christian beliefs, as seen in Aslan's sacrifice. They have some features of fairy tales, such as dwarfs and witches, and also contain creatures from Classical mythology, such as **dryads**, **centaurs**, and **satyrs**. Lewis was also inspired by epic poetry. The voyage of the *Dawn Treader* echoes the voyage in an Ancient Greek storypoem called *The Odyssey*.

Satyrs have the top half of a man, with the legs and horns of a goat.

The end of a great life

Lewis remained unwell, and in April 1962 he decided to return to Cambridge University anyway. He compiled his lectures into a book called *The Discarded Image* and wrote a book on praying called *Letters to Malcolm*. Early in the summer vacation of 1963, Lewis was at a nursing home having a blood transfusion when he had a heart attack. It left him very weak, and in August Lewis **resigned** from the university. On 22 November 1963, he died peacefully at home, aged nearly 65.

Having lived through World War I, Lewis died in his old age. He had fulfilled his wartime promise to Paddy Moore by taking care of Mrs Moore at The Kilns.

FIND OUT MORE...

In a lecture in 1952, Lewis said: "a children's story which is enjoyed only by children is a bad children's story. The good ones last..." Years after his death, the popularity of Lewis's *Chronicles of Narnia* shows no sign of fading, and the stories are loved by readers of all ages.

LEWIS'S WRITING

Lewis lived his life in a hurry, never wanting to waste a minute when he could be writing. He usually had an early, quick breakfast and went for a walk, then made sure he was back in his college rooms at nine o'clock to do an hour's writing before his first pupil of the day arrived at ten. Besides one-to-one teaching, Lewis also had to give lectures to groups of students. These were held in a building called the Examination Schools on the High Street. Lewis's lectures were usually packed, because the students thought he was an outstanding teacher. Lewis always rushed in and out at top speed. He usually started speaking before he had even come properly through the door and finished talking as he strode off down the corridor. He never hung about to give the students the opportunity to delay him with questions. Lewis needed as much time for his writing as possible.

How did Lewis write?

Lewis always wrote **longhand**, using a fountain pen and ink. If he was working on an academic book, he often went over and over his writing, rethinking and revising it. However, when he was working on fiction, he usually got it right first time, hardly ever making corrections. When his **manuscripts** were typed up and sent to publishers, he used his original, handwritten copies for scrap paper.

INSIDE INFORMATION

Lewis once said: "I wrote the books I should have liked to read if only I could have got them. That's always been my reason for writing. People won't write the books I want, so I have to do it for myself…"

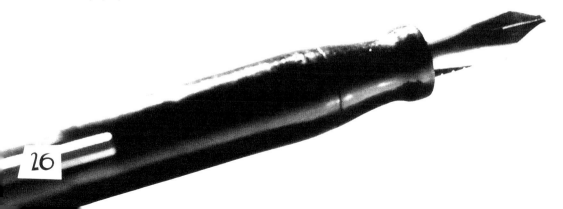

Where did Lewis write?

Lewis did most of his writing in his college rooms. When he was teaching at Magdalen College, Oxford, he often went home to The Kilns for lunch but slept in college overnight so that he could stay up late, writing. Lewis loved his rooms at Magdalen College. His furniture was shabby, but comfy. He wrote at a large table in the middle of the main room, which also had battered armchairs in front of the fireplace. Off this main room were a bedroom and another little room where Lewis kept his small collection of books.

Lewis spent endless hours happily writing in his rooms at Magdalen College in Oxford.

THE CHRONICLES OF NARNIA

Main characters

Aslan...................... a mighty lion – the creator of Narnia
Peter, Susan,
  Edmund, and
  Lucy Pevensie..... siblings who become rulers of Narnia
Digory Kirke .... a boy who becomes "the Professor"
Polly Plummer........ Digory's childhood neighbour and friend
Uncle Andrew .... Digory's uncle, an amateur magician
Queen Jadis.......... who becomes the White Witch
Mr Tumnus .... a faun, Lucy's firm friend
Prince Caspian .... who becomes a great King of Narnia
Trumpkin .... a dwarf – trusted friend of Caspian
Reepicheep .... a noble, knightly mouse
Eustace Scrubb...... the Pevensie children's cousin
Jill Pole.................. Eustace's school friend
Puddleglum........... a marshwiggle – and reluctant hero
Shasta..................... a penniless boy, who is also
                       a long-lost prince
Prince Corin .... Shasta's twin brother
Aravis .... a noblewoman from Calormen
Bree and Hwin ...... two talking horses
Shift and Puzzle..... a cunning ape and a gullible donkey
King Tirian .... a loyal young man – the last King of Narnia
Jewel .... King Tirian's courageous unicorn friend

THE LION, THE WITCH AND THE WARDROBE

The plot

The Pevensie children are staying with an old Professor in his country house. Lucy discovers a way through a wardrobe into the magical country of Narnia. An evil White Witch is in charge, turning creatures into stone, and ensuring it is always winter but never Christmas. Edmund falls into her clutches and turns traitor. Only Aslan can rescue Edmund and free Narnia – but at a terrible price.

INSIDE INFORMATION

Lewis said that his starting point for *The Lion, the Witch and the Wardrobe* was a picture that popped into his head when he was sixteen, of a faun carrying an umbrella and parcels in a snowy wood. He began writing the tale with little idea of what might happen in it, and with no plans for any others.

THE LION, THE WITCH
and
THE WARDROBE

A Story for Children
by
C. S. LEWIS

The Lion, the Witch and the Wardrobe was published in 1950. It was Lewis's first book for children.

PRINCE CASPIAN

The plot

The Pevensie children are sitting at a railway station when they find themselves pulled by magic into Narnia. Prince Caspian has called them because he desperately needs their help. His murdering uncle, Miraz, has silenced Narnia's talking animals and driven all the other magical creatures out of the country. Caspian is determined to claim his rightful throne and restore Narnia to its former glory. Will the former Kings and Queens of Narnia be able to help him win a bloody **civil war**?

INSIDE INFORMATION

The first part of this tale that Lewis thought of was its very unusual beginning. Instead of describing what it was like to be someone summoning up people by magic, Lewis described what it was like to be the people summoned. Lewis originally called the story "Drawn into Narnia".

PRINCE CASPIAN
The Return to Narnia

A Story for Children
by
C. S. LEWIS

Prince Caspian was published in 1951.

THE VOYAGE OF THE DAWN TREADER

The plot

Edmund and Lucy Pevensie and Eustace Scrubb fall through a painting onto the royal Narnian ship, the *Dawn Treader*. They find themselves on a voyage with King Caspian into the unknown waters of the Eastern Seas. He is searching for seven of his father's friends who vanished long ago beyond the Lone Islands. Also on board is Reepicheep, who is on a personal quest to travel beyond the end of the world and discover Aslan's own country.

The Voyage of the Dawn Treader was published in 1952.

THE VOYAGE OF THE DAWN TREADER

A Story for Children
by
C. S. LEWIS

INSIDE INFORMATION

Lewis was passionate about Medieval literature. It often included tales about gallant knights who went on courageous missions to do valiant deeds and win honour, in the face of death. Reepicheep the mouse is such a character. He is described as "the most valiant of all the Talking Beasts of Narnia".

THE SILVER CHAIR

The plot

Eustace Scrubb and Jill Pole are trying to escape from school bullies when they discover a way into Narnia. Aslan sets them the task of finding the aged King Caspian's lost son, Prince Rilian. With the help of Puddleglum the marshwiggle, they make a dangerous journey far from the safety of Narnia, through the land of giants, Ettinsmoor, into the deep, dark realm of the Earthmen, Underland. Then there are powerful enchantments to break.

The Silver Chair was published in 1953.

A Story for Children
by
C. S. LEWIS

INSIDE INFORMATION

Lewis based the character of Puddleglum on his gardener at The Kilns, Fred Paxford. He was a gloomy man who enjoyed singing solemn hymns very loudly. He was fiercely loyal to Lewis and worked at The Kilns from 1930 until Lewis died – over 30 years' service.

THE HORSE AND HIS BOY

The plot

Shasta lives in a land neighbouring Narnia called Calormen. He discovers that the fisherman he has always believed is his father is in fact not his father at all, and runs away. Shasta meets an enslaved talking horse, Bree, and together they set off for a new life in Narnia. They meet a noblewoman on another talking horse, also on the run, and begin a journey to self-discovery as well as freedom.

INSIDE INFORMATION

Lewis had a respectful attitude towards animals. He believed that people had a responsibility to look after animals, but should at the same time allow them to be as wild and natural as possible. He once wrote in a letter that in an ideal world "if you wanted a horse to ride, you would walk up to the nearest herd and ask for volunteers".

THE HORSE
AND
HIS BOY

A Story for Children
by
C. S. LEWIS

The Horse and his Boy was published in 1954.

THE MAGICIAN'S NEPHEW

The plot

Digory and Polly stumble across Uncle Andrew's secret attic workroom. Uncle Andrew forces them to take part in one of his magic experiments and sends them off into the unknown. But Uncle Andrew does not bargain on Digory and Polly bringing back a powerful, wicked sorceress from a dying planet. And he never imagines that he himself will be whisked away to witness the creation of a brand new world, Narnia.

INSIDE INFORMATION

Lewis began writing The Magician's Nephew straight after finishing The Lion, the Witch and the Wardrobe. He wanted to think about where the White Witch came from and how the lamp post came to be in Narnia. However, Lewis got stuck with the story and turned to other Narnia tales instead. The Magician's Nephew was eventually the sixth Narnia story published, but it should be read first in the series.

The Magician's Nephew was published in 1955.

A Story for Children by
C. S. LEWIS

THE LAST BATTLE

The plot

Shift, the ape, dresses Puzzle, the donkey, in a lion skin, and passes him off as Aslan. Shift uses his new-found power for evil ends, felling tree spirits, enslaving talking animals, and spreading terrible lies. King Tirian and his unicorn friend, Jewel, are determined to stop the wickedness destroying their country. Tirian desperately calls on the human friends of Narnia to help. But even these heroes and heroines from the past cannot overcome the evil that has taken hold in Narnia this time. And where is the real Aslan, when Narnia needs him most?

The Last Battle was published in 1956.

THE
LAST BATTLE

A Story for Children by
C. S. LEWIS

INSIDE INFORMATION

Aslan refers to Narnia and Earth as "shadowlands". He means they are changing, shifting worlds that can fade and die, in comparison to heaven – which lasts forever. The word "shadowlands" was later used as the title for the film of Lewis's life.

PRIZES, PERFORMANCE, PRAISE

Before Lewis's *Chronicles of Narnia* became children's best-sellers, he was already famous all over the world as a writer for adults. He was given many honours through his lifetime for his religious books and for his outstanding academic work. *The Allegory of Love* won the Gollancz Memorial Prize for Literature. Lewis was given the title of **Honorary** Doctor of Divinity from St Andrews University and the title of Honorary Doctor of Literature from Manchester University. He was made an important member called a Fellow of two leading arts societies: the British Academy and the Royal Society of Literature. The Queen also wanted to give Lewis the title of CBE (Commander of the Order of the British Empire), although he politely refused the honour. He did not like accepting awards that were in any way political.

The success of the Narnia books

Lewis won one of the top honours in children's publishing: the Carnegie Medal. He was awarded it in 1956 for *The Last Battle*. Since then, the seven books that make up *The Chronicles of Narnia* have sold over 90 million copies worldwide, have appeared in countless editions including audio, and have been translated into over 40 languages.

Other writers who have won the Carnegie Medal include Philip Pullman, Jan Mark, Terry Pratchett, and Anne Fine.

Narnia on stage

Several theatre companies have turned *The Lion, the Witch and the Wardrobe* into a play. The most well-known version was a musical production by the Royal Shakespeare Company in England. It was first performed in 1998, when it broke box office records. When it was performed in 2000, it was so popular that the company sold over £1.3 million worth of tickets before the first performance!

The Royal Shakespeare Company stage version of *The Lion, the Witch and the Wardrobe* was very popular with both children and adults.

If you want to turn a Narnia story or other favourite tale into a play or a musical, here are some things to think about:

- How will you tell your audience what your characters are thinking and feeling inside? You can do this entirely through your characters' dialogue and action, or you could have a character who occasionally speaks directly to the audience, or a **narrator**.

- How will you handle the timescale of your story? A play usually starts at the beginning of a story and works its way through to the end in time order. If you want to add some twists, you can have "flashback" scenes of the past or "dream" scenes of the future.

- How will you arrange the different parts of the story into a sequence? Try to break the action up into scenes that take place in different settings. You need to make sure that you do not have too many settings if you are writing a play for the stage, otherwise you will need too much scenery.

- Try to make your characters' speech realistic so the audience will believe what is happening.

- You can include brief instructions to the actors in your script too, to tell them how you want them to speak their lines (for instance, "angrily" or "whispering") and what they should be doing (for example, "he stomps upstairs" or "she creeps in the shadows").

- To make action scenes exciting, you can use special lighting effects and stunts.

Narnia on screen

Over the years, the Narnia stories have been read aloud on BBC Radio 4, and have appeared in different versions on television. In 1967, ABC Television produced a **dramatized** series of *The Lion, the Witch and the Wardrobe* in nine, twenty-minute instalments. The programmes were black and white, as all television was then. In 1976, two American companies joined together to make a long, **animated** film of *The Lion, the Witch and the Wardrobe*, which was also broadcast in Britain. The BBC produced lavish television dramatizations of *The Lion, the Witch and the Wardrobe*, *Prince Caspian*, *The Voyage of the Dawn Treader*, and *The Silver Chair* in the late 1980s.

In 2005, Disney released the first Hollywood movie version of *The Lion, the Witch and the Wardrobe* – an exciting big-screen blockbuster with stars including Jim Broadbent, Tilda Swinton, Rupert Everett, Dawn French, and Ray Winstone.

These young actors play Edmund, Peter, Lucy and Susan in the 2005 Disney movie *The Lion, the Witch and the Wardrobe*.

Views in the news

Lewis's Narnia stories won praise from many critics. These are people paid to write their opinions of books. Book reviews are important because they help readers decide whether to spend their time and money on a story or not. Here is an example of a review for *The Chronicles of Narnia*, with some notes on how the critic has put it together. Would it encourage you to read the books?

The *Chronicles of Narnia* is a masterpiece by C.S. Lewis, who was a teacher at Oxford University who also wrote famous books for adults.

some background on the writer

The *Chronicles* consist of seven tales about a world of talking animals and magical creatures, Narnia, from its creation to its destruction. We follow the adventures of children from our world who stumble across unexpected ways into Narnia and bravely undertake dangerous quests.

a summary of what kind of books they are

Lewis wrote the *Chronicles* in the 1950s, and although some of the language now seems dated, the characters are still as captivating today as they were then, and the lessons the children learn are just as important. For years, girls and boys of eight and upwards have been enchanted by these classic novels, and older readers delight in recognizing deeper meanings in the stories.

the critic's opinion on whether it is a good or bad read, with clear reasons why

who the work is aimed at

No matter what your age, if you like fantasy stories with a strong sense of good and evil, *The Chronicles of Narnia* are the originals and the best.

a recommendation of who the critic thinks will like the book

HAVE A GO

Why not try writing a review of one of the Narnia stories? You could give it to a friend who does not know the tale and see if they go on to read it. Ask them to write a review back, recommending one of their favourite books to you. You might discover your new favourite book, poem, or author...

Pieces of praise

Here are some critics' opinions on Lewis's work:

"Nothing he wrote has captured the imaginations of more children and adults than the seven books that make up *The Chronicles of Narnia*."

New York Times

"His words have altered lives."
Time magazine

"Commonly regarded as one of the best children's books of all time."

The Scotsman

"Lewis's writing takes on a life of its own ... highly recommended."

Library Journal

"...glimpses of another world older, deeper and more magical than this one."

The Independent

If you would like to walk in Lewis's footsteps, you can visit the grounds of both Magdalen College, Oxford, and Magdalene College, Cambridge. The garden at Lewis's home, The Kilns, is always open to visitors and you can make an appointment to look around the house itself. At Lewis's church, Holy Trinity in Headington, Oxford, you can find not only Lewis's gravestone but also a Narnia window that was installed there in 1991.

Lewis was buried near his home in Oxford. Narnia fans often come to visit his grave.

Lewis's legacy

The Chronicles of Narnia have enjoyed such enormous, lasting success that publishers are considering asking authors to create new tales based in Lewis's magical world. Writers have also composed new Screwtape letters. Lewis's wonderful work will no doubt continue to inspire generations to come.

Writing in focus

Here's what some of Lewis's millions of fans worldwide think about him and his work:

"I have read my Narnia books so many times that the pages are falling out!"

Lorna, 12, from Belfast, Northern Ireland

"The Narnia books are the greatest fantasy series of all time."

Zac, 13, from New York, the USA

"Lucy is my favourite ever story character. I wish we could be friends."

Nancy, 10, from Birmingham, England

LEWIS'S WISH LIST

Hopes...	Lewis hoped to see his novel, *Perelandra*, turned into an opera. After Joy died, he worked on this project with composers. Unfortunately, he did not live to see the first performance.
Dreams...	As a young man, Lewis dreamed of becoming a poet – as did his close friend, J.R.R. Tolkien. In the end, they both won worldwide fame for writing novels and other prose instead.
Ambitions...	In 1952, Lewis said in a lecture: "I am not quite sure what made me in a particular year of my life, feel that not only a fairy tale, but a fairy tale addressed to children, was exactly what I must write." *The Chronicles of Narnia* was a magnificent achievement of this ambition.

TIMELINE

1898 Clive Staples Lewis is born on 29 November in Belfast, Northern Ireland.

1905 Lewis's family move to a house called Little Lea on the outskirts of Belfast.

1908 Lewis's mother dies. Lewis is sent away to boarding school.

1914 World War I breaks out.

1915 Lewis starts writing poetry.
He wins a scholarship to attend Oxford University.

1917 Lewis starts studying at University College, Oxford University.
He also trains as an army officer. He is sent to France to fight in World War I on 17 November.

1918 Lewis is wounded in March and sent to hospital in England.
World War I ends in November. His friend Paddy Moore has been killed in the fighting.

1919 Lewis returns to his studies at Oxford University in January.
A book of Lewis's poems, called *Spirits in Bondage*, is published.

1921 Lewis rents a house to share with Paddy's mother and sister, Maureen. He wins a university essay prize.

1922 Lewis achieves the highest grade in his university Classics degree.

1923 Lewis achieves a very high grade in his English degree.
He begins teaching at University College, Oxford University.

1925 Lewis takes up an English teaching job called a Fellowship, at Magdalen College, Oxford University.

1926 Lewis writes a variety of poetry and academic books.
Lewis also meets J.R.R. Tolkien and goes to meetings of the Coalbiters' Club to read Old Icelandic literature.

1929 Lewis's father dies. Lewis and his brother, Warnie, sell Little Lea.

1930 Lewis and Warnie move in to a house they have bought together in Headington, Oxford. Mrs Moore and Maureen move in too.

1933 *The Pilgrim's Regress* is published.

1935 Lewis, Tolkien and other writer friends meet regularly to discuss their work. They call themselves the Inklings.

1936	*The Allegory of Love* is published.
1938	*Out of the Silent Planet* is published.
1939	World War II begins. Lewis, aged 40, joins the Home Guard.
1940	*The Problem of Pain* is published. Lewis becomes very well-known for giving talks on BBC radio, at Royal Air Force bases, and in churches.
1941	*The Screwtape Letters* appear in serial form in *The Guardian* newspaper.
1942	*The Screwtape Letters* are published as a book in the UK.
1943	*The Screwtape Letters* are published as a book in the US. Lewis becomes famous internationally. With money he gets for the book, he sets up a trust fund to help poor people.
1945	World War II ends.
1950	*The Lion, the Witch and the Wardrobe* is published.
1951	*Prince Caspian* is published.
1952	*The Voyage of the Dawn Treader* is published. Lewis meets Joy Davidman and they become friends.
1953	*The Silver Chair* is published.
1954	*The Horse and his Boy* is published. Lewis takes up the position of Professor of Medieval and Renaissance English at Cambridge University.
1955	*The Magician's Nephew* is published.
1956	*The Last Battle* is published and wins the Carnegie Medal. Lewis marries Joy Davidman. They discover she is dying.
1960	Joy dies.
1961	Lewis continues to write but in the summer, he falls ill. He has to take time off from university teaching.
1962	Lewis remains unwell, but returns to university teaching.
1963	Lewis has to resign from Cambridge University because of his poor health.
1963	Lewis dies on 22 November, aged nearly 65.

FURTHER RESOURCES

More books to read

C.S. Lewis: A Biography, Roger Lancelyn Green and Walter Hooper (HarperCollins, 2003)

Pocket Companion to Narnia: A Concise Guide to the Magical World of C.S. Lewis, Paul F. Ford (ZonderKidz, 2005)

So You Think You Know Narnia, Clive Gifford (Hodder Children's Books, 2005)

The Lion, the Witch and the Wardrobe Movie Storybook (HarperCollins Children's Books, 2005)

Audio and video

The Chronicles of Narnia are also available as audiobooks on CD and cassette:

Complete Chronicles of Narnia (BBC Audiobooks, 2000)

The Chronicles of Narnia series (HarperCollins, 2005)

The BBC television adaptations of Lewis's stories are available on DVD and video:

The Chronicles of Narnia (BBC, 2005)

Websites

This site is for fans of Narnia and C.S. Lewis:
www.narniafans.com

A site all about books for young people:
www.booktrusted.co.uk

academic to do with education and studying

allegory piece of work that has a more obvious surface layer of meaning, but also a "hidden" layer of meaning underneath

allies countries that agree to fight on the same side during a war

animated given the illusion of movement

cancer serious illlness which can kill people

Celtic relating to the Celts, an ancient group of people who lived in parts of Britain and much of Europe thousands of years ago

centaur creature from Greek myths that is half man, half horse

civil war war that takes place between groups of people within the same country

Classics study of important writing from ancient civilizations, such as the Romans and Greeks

degree qualification that students work for at university

dramatized acted out

dryad tree spirit

epic ancient form of storytelling, focusing on heroes and their adventures

evacuee child sent from their home in a city during a war to stay in the countryside where it was safer

fantasy story set in an imaginary, magical world

fiction imaginative writing, such as stories, rather than information writing

governess female teacher employed by a family to work at home, teaching the children

honorary something given to honour someone

lawyer person who practises law

longhand writing on paper with a pen or pencil rather than typing

manuscript author's original typed or written version of their book

medieval period of European history which lasted from the 11th to the 15th century

myth traditional story from early history, typically about gods, goddesses, spirits, and heroes

narrator person who tells a story

Renaissance period of European history which lasted from the 14th to the 17th century

resign give up a job or a position

satyr creature from myths which is half man, half goat

scholarship prize of money to help a student pay the fees for a course of study

science fiction story based on science and technology but with made-up elements, often set in a different time or place

trench ditch dug on a battlefield for soldiers to shelter in and to shoot at the enemy from

INDEX

Titles in the *Writers Uncovered* series include:

Hardback   0 431 90626 2

Hardback   0 431 90627 0

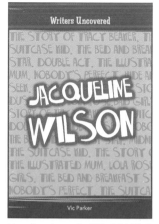

Hardback   0 431 90628 9

Hardback   0 431 90629 7

Hardback   0 431 90630 0

Hardback   0 431 90631 9

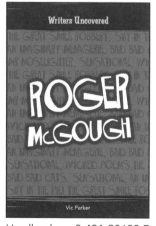

Hardback   0 431 90632 7

Hardback   0 431 90633 5

Find out about other titles from Heinemann Library on our website www.heinemann.co.uk/library